InSite Performance in association with Leeds Playhouse

BLACKTHORN
by Charley Miles

Blackthorn was originally produced by
Leeds Playhouse for Furnace Festival 2016.

With support from Cleveland Steel, McCormacks Law
and Arts Council England

BLACKTHORN
by Charley Miles

Cast

HER	**Charlotte Bate**
HIM	**Harry Egan**

Company

Director	**Jacqui Honess-Martin**
Producer	**Rowan Rutter**
Movement Director	**Natasha Harrison**
Lighting Designer	**Jose Tevar**
Composer	**Heather Fenoughty**

Blackthorn was revived at
Paines Plough's Roundabout at Summerhall,
Edinburgh Festival Fringe
1–26 August 2018

Biographies

Harry Egan | HIM

Harry trained at Bristol Old Vic Theatre School. Theatre credits include *One Flew Over the Cuckoo's Nest* (Sheffield Crucible); *Of Mice and Men* (Selladoor UK tour); *Breaking the Code* (Royal Exchange, Manchester); Him in *Blackthorn* (Leeds Playhouse); *The Tiger's Bones* (New Perspectives); *The Wars of the Roses* (Rose Theatre).

Charlotte Bate | HER

Charlotte trained at the Guildhall School of Music and Drama. Theatre credits include Julia in *The Rivals*, Kehar/Thethuthinanng in *Watership Down* (Watermill Theatre); Goneril in *King Lear* (Orange Tree, Richmond); Her in *Blackthorn* (Leeds Playhouse); Friar Laurence in *Romeo and Juliet* (Sheffield Crucible).

Charley Miles | Writer

Charley Miles' debut play is *Blackthorn*, a brilliantly lyrical, expansive two-hander that premiered at the Leeds Playhouse in September 2016. *Blackthorn* was a 2016-2017 finalist for the Susan Smith Blackburn Prize. *Spilt* was commissioned by the Royal Court and Royal Welsh College of Music and Drama and was performed in Cardiff and at the Gate Theatre London in 2018. Charley was Channel 4 Writer in Residence at Leeds Playhouse in 2017 and is Paines Plough Fellow, 2018. Charley is from Kilburn, North Yorkshire.

Jacqui Honess-Martin | Director

Jacqui is a playwright and director. She has been the Literary Associate at Leeds Playhouse since 2015. For InSite Performance she has directed *Abyss*, *Larisa and the Merchants* (Arcola Theatre); *We Have Fallen* (Underbelly Edinburgh, writer and director); *SMITH* (writer and director) and *Antigone* (adaptor and director). Other directing credits include *Blackthorn* (Leeds Playhouse); *Atman* by Iain Finlay Macleod (Finborough); *Auricular* (Theatre503) and *Necessary Evil* by Ben Askew (Menagerie Theatre Company, The Junction, Cambridge). She has directed at Drama Centre, London and RADA. She was Staff Director on the UK Tour of *People* by Alan Bennett for the National Theatre. Her assisting credits include *Arcadia* (West End); *Remembrance Day* and *The Faith Machine* (Royal Court). Her playwriting credits include *Pine* (Hampstead Theatre in 2015 and *Tell Out My Soul* (Public Theatre New York, 2008).

Rowan Rutter | Producer

Rowan is currently Executive Producer for Avant Garde Dance. Other productions include *Atlantis* and *Young Blood! Kommilitonen* (operas) with Loud Crowd in association with Bold Tendencies. As Producer for Hull Truck Theatre she produced the Year of Exceptional Drama for Hull UK City of Culture 2017, including the Royal Shakespeare Company (Richard Bean's *The Hypocrite*); Northern Broadsides (Shakespeare's *Richard III*); and an international tour of the Market Theatre, Johannesburg production of *The Suitcase*. Previously Rowan has worked with Clean Break, Cardboard Citizens and Barely Methodical Troupe.

Natasha Harrison | Movement Director

Trained at Northern School of Contemporary Dance and Royal Central School of Speech and Drama. Theatre includes *Julius Caesar* (RSC - First Encounters); *Building the Wall* (Park Theatre); *Yokes Night* (Theatre Royal Stratford East); *Zoetrope, Ode to Leeds, Blackthorn, Into the woods* (West Yorkshire Playhouse); *Sacha Guitry: Ma Fille et Moi* (Drayton Arms); *Tumulus* (VAULT Festival); *Tiny Dynamite* (Old Red Lion); *Dear Brutus, The Cardinal* (Southwark Playhouse); *Leeds Lads* (The Carriageworks, Leeds); *The Taming of the Shrew* (Webber Douglas Studio). Associate Choreography includes *Birds of Paradise* (The Ingénue Magazine). Opera includes *The Lighthouse, The Locked Room, Les Mamelles de Tirésias, Une Éducation Manquée* (Royal College of Music). Natasha is the BA Dance and Movement Lecturer at the Leeds Beckett University and Guest Movement Lecturer at the Royal College of Music.

Jose Tevar | Lighting Designer

Jose is a freelance lighting designer from Hull. Jose studied MA Design for Performance (Lighting) at the Royal Welsh College of Music and Drama and has worked as a lighting technician for Hull Truck Theatre and Royal Caribbean International. Jose has recently designed for National Dance Company Wales, and will be designing Middle Child's *All We Ever Wanted Was Everything* at the Bush Theatre in November. Recent lighting design credits include *Betty Blue Eyes* (Richard Burton Theatre, 2018); NDCW's *Alternative Routes* (Dance House, 2018); *La Cenerentola* (Dora Stoutzker Concert Hall, 2018), and Middle Child's *One Life Stand* (tour, 2018).

Heather Fenoughty | Composer

Heather Fenoughty is an award-winning composer and sound designer for theatre, film, television, games and multimedia. Music and sound design includes Slung Low's *Flood* (RTS Yorkshire Award for Production Excellence); Third Angel's *Department of Distractions* and *Partus*; *The Count of Monte Cristo* (West Yorkshire Playhouse); Slung Low's productions of *Camelot: The Shining City* (Crucible); *Emergency Story Penguin* (Crucible); *The White Whale* (Leeds Dock); *Blood + Chocolate*

(York Theatre Royal); *They Only Come at Night: Pandemic* (Singapore Arts Festival); *Converging Paths*; *59 Minutes to Save Christmas* (Barbican); *Mapping The City* (Hull Truck); *Anthology* (Liverpool Playhouse); *Last Seen* (Almeida); *Beyond the Front Line* (Lowry) and *Helium* (OSBTT/Barbican) and as composer and MD of the band in Slung Low's regular *15 Minutes Live* series. She scored *'Tis Pity She's A Whore* for the Liverpool Playhouse and her music for *Terre Haute* (Nabokov,) played on the West End and Off-Broadway. Television credits include scores for several feature films, documentaries, animations and short films broadcast on the BBC and ITV networks. Commercial credits include adverts for Nissan and CITV, and her production library music has featured on *The Daily Show*, *CNN* and *CBS News*. Heather was Composer-in-Residence for the Arthur C. Clarke Awards 2009, and creates production library tracks for Premiumbeat.

InSite Performance produces new writing, driven by an all-female Artistic/Producing Team, telling female-led narratives that have been overlooked.

The portfolio includes *Larisa and the Merchant*s (Samuel Adamson), *Abyss* (Maria Milisavljevic), *We Have Fallen* (Jacqui Honess-Martin) – all directed by Jacqui Honess-Martin and produced by Rowan Rutter.

We have presented UK premieres of work by international writers and have presented work at the Arcola Theatre, Theatre503, the Finborough Theatre, Underbelly and in site-specific locations, including the British Museum.

insiteperformance.com

InSite Performance Ltd. is a registered charity: 1148573

Welcome to the home of incredible stories

There has been a Playhouse in Leeds for almost fifty years; from 1968 to 1990 as Leeds Playhouse and then with the opening of a brand new theatre on its current Quarry Hill site it became West Yorkshire Playhouse.

Leeds Playhouse is a leading UK producing theatre; a cultural hub, a place where people gather to tell and share stories and to engage in world class theatre. We make work which is pioneering and relevant, seeking out the best companies and artists to create inspirational theatre in the heart of Yorkshire. From large-scale spectacle to intimate performance we develop and make work for our stages, for found spaces, for touring, for schools and community centres. We create work to entertain and inspire.

As dedicated collaborators, we work regularly with other organisations from across the UK, independent producers, and some of the most distinctive, original voices in theatre today. Through our Furnace programme, we develop work with established practitioners and find, nurture and support new voices that ought to be heard. We cultivate artists by providing creative space for writers, directors, companies and individual theatre makers to refine their practice at any stage of their career.

Alongside our work for the stage we are dedicated to providing creative engagement opportunities that excite and stimulate. We build, run and sustain projects which reach out to everyone from refugee communities, to young people and students, to older communities and people with learning disabilities. At the Playhouse there is always a way to get involved.

Leeds Playhouse – Vital Theatre

Artistic Director **James Brining**
Executive Director **Robin Hawkes**
Chairman of the Board **Sir Rodney Brooke CBE**
Find us on Facebook: **Leeds Playhouse**
Follow us on Twitter: **@LeedsPlayhouse**
Follow us on Instagram: **@LeedsPlayhouse**

LeedsPlayhouse.org.uk

Leeds Theatre Trust Limited Charity Number 255460
VAT No. 545 4890 17 Company No. 926862, England Wales
Registered address Playhouse Square, Quarry Hill, Leeds, LS2 7UP

BLACKTHORN

Charley Miles

For Kilburn
everyone and everywhere that made me

Thanks

This play was born out of the lifelong support of some, and the more recent encouragement of others.

Thanks to Gilly, Sophie, James, Robin, and all at Leeds Playhouse for first believing in it and in me, and giving the play its first breath of life; to Harry Egan and Charlie Bate, for their exquisite talents and instincts; to Matt Hartley for his selfless support, and Paines Plough for the new life; to Marnie Podos, for her brilliance and enthusiasm.

Special thanks to my mum and dad, for their endless support. We might not have understood what we were getting ourselves into, but your unquestioning belief made it feel possible. To Izzy, for being my first reader, always; to Eve, for being easy to make laugh; to Frankie, for his love.

Thanks to the volley of female friends who support me through everything. Most especially, to Tashan Mehta, my sister-in-arms and most wise adviser: I could not understand myself without you.

This play would not have been possible without the relentless encouragement, energy and wisdom of Jacqui Honess-Martin. Thank you for your rigour and insight—for giving me reasons to aim higher.

C.M.

Characters

HER
HIM

A forward slash (/) indicates when the next line begins.

This edition features the full-length version of the play.
A shortened version was first performed at the Edinburgh
Festival Fringe.

This text went to press before the end of rehearsals and so may
differ slightly from the play as performed.

HER   When we get born
      we're the first babies born for twenty years.

HIM   They tell us

HER   they love to tell us

HIM   about how it's not the same.

HER   You can move here at six years old or sixty
      or even six weeks newborn.

HIM   But it's not the same.

HER   No.
      It's not the same as us.

HER   This time –
HIM   they're panting
HER   heavily.
HIM   As though they've just run a

HER   Let's play something different than horses now.

HIM   Want to race sticks in beck?

HER   I think we should play a game of mummies and daddies.

HIM   That's a girl's game.

HER   No it's not cos it's got mummies AND daddies in it
        stupid.
        So's I'll be the / mummy.

HIM   Could catch for minnows?

HER   And you be the daddy. And you're like
        What do you want to be?

HIM   I don't want to be the daddy.

HER   You have to be the daddy.
        And you can pick what you want to do for work and
        I think I'll
        I think that I should

HIM   You have to look after the babies.

HER   I haven't had any babies yet we're going to make the
        babies in a bit.

HIM   Can I be a pirate?

HER   You can't be a pirate in real life.

HIM   There are pirates in real life.

HER   You could just be a sailor if you like?

HIM   I want a parrot.

HER   You could work like
        you could do what Tom's dad does
        and you could go out to the sea for the long time and

on the
On the
Looking for oil.
That's a sort of pirate?

HIM   Is Tom's dad a pirate?

HER   Yeh. Sort of. He told me.
So you be a
Going out onto the oils for the long time
which means we have to have a really big fight.

HIM   Why?

HER   Cos you didn't got your other job that you used to
have. You lost it.

HIM   How do you lose a job?

HER   I don't know. Just being really careless, I think.
I can't believe you lost your job! Being really careless!
I hate you!

HIM   I hate you too!!

HER   No! You have to
You have to be like oh but I love you and I'm sorry
and please.
And kiss me now.

HIM   Yuck!!!!!! Why?????

HER   You have to make me love you again.

HIM   I never want to kiss a girl in my whole life ever. I made
a promise about it. Never. Ever.

HER   You kiss your mum.

HIM   Don't.

HER   Seen you.

HIM   Yeah well. She's the only one. Only cos I have to.

HER   You do have to, cos it's part of the game.

         –

HIM   I don't have to marry you, do I?

HER   You don't have to get married if you have a kiss,
        stupid. My auntie's always kissing loads of boys and
        she's never even been married once.

HIM   Fine.
        But only if you close your eyes.
        And I'm be closing mine too.

        –

        YUCK YUCK YUCK YUCK YUCK
        And you opened your eyes, you cheater!

HER   Okay so I'm probably going to work now. Now you're
        out on the oils.

HIM   I hate this game!

HER   Okay well I think that you just needs to calm down.
        What d'you want to play then? Hey?
        D'you want to play horses again?

HIM   Yeah and I'll be the stag.

HER   That's not a horse.

HIM   It is it's the boy one that they let
        they let him keep his you know.
        Only one does get to and he's special cos then he gets
        to have babies with all the mares.
        I seen it. Seen it when his thing's out.

HER   His WILLY?

HIM   Shut up!! So's I'll be stag cos you know

HER   I don't think it's fair that you get to be stag because
        you got born with
        Girls should get willies too.

HIM   You get something different though.

HER   Do you get it when you're older?

HIM   What?

HER   What we get instead of a willy. Do we get it when
        we're older?

HIM   Think you get born with it, same.

HER   But I don't have anything.

HIM   I seen my mum's.

HER   What's it look like??

HIM   It's just a bit hairy.

HER   Do you want to
        shall we swap looking? Just really quickly.

HIM   Get in trouble.

HER   But we could
        go behind the hedge.

HIM   –

HER   Shall I take my knickers off?

HIM   No we'll do it later maybe. At home and
        behind the sofa.

HER   Okay. So
        I'm going to be a
        probably be a horse-racer

HIM   Can't be the racer if we're both horses, can you?
        Otherwise it just
        it can't make sense!!

HER   Anyway I don't want to be a horse any more.
        I want to be the daddy. I'll go out to the oils.

HIM   But we're not playing that game any more.

HER   So I'm the daddy out on the oils
        You make the tea. Or let's
        Actually let's be like
        you be John Smith

HIM   Out on the oils?

HER   No stupid he's a different sort of sailor so I'm
        I'm like running in the wind and

HIM   I'm going in now.

HER   No but I'm like running all in the wind / and

HIM   I SAID I'm going in now.

HER   –
       Why??

HIM   You ent playing properly.
       You have to just pick one thing. To be.

HER   Well sorry…

HIM   You can't change your mind all the time cos it's just
       really confusing in the game and it'll make people just
       not want to play with you any more.

       –

HER   I'm going into the barn then.
       Going to climb the haystacks.

HIM   You aren't.

HER   I am.

HIM   It's dangerous.

HER   I think that if we're friends then we should just
       probably do it together so you come along wi' me now.
       Come on. You come and play wi' me. And I'm going
       in there.

       –

       A little boy died that climbed in the haystacks once.

HIM   You didn't even know him it was a long time
       It was before
       It was when you was still a star in the sky.

HER   Yeah but I know
       cos he's my cousin. I get really sad about it but
       I'll show you.

       –

HIM   You're not allowed.

HER   Yeah well d'you know that
       like I do know all about it all how it happened.
       I know what happens when people die.
       He died by a
       Tragedy.

HIM   My dad told me but you wasn't told cos you was too
       young.
       When we got told off for it. For climbing.
       I wasn't 'llowed to tell you, but I got told.

HER   No you don't cos
       he was my cousin he actually was.

HIM   He climbed up and then all the bales fell down on him
       and all on his face
       and in his mouth
       and like when you put your head under the bath
       and he couldn't even breathe.

       –

HER   Like
       a bath?

HIM   You come away now. I'm older than you so I'm
       looking after you.

       –

HER   He my cousin, he was.
       I'm really sad about it now. You ent got nothing to be
       sad about.
       And I'm going in there
       to be
       to remember him by.
       I'll probably get a smack but
       I'm very brave.

       –

HIM   I'll tell.
       I will.

HER   No you won't tell on.

HIM   –

HER   –

HIM   You hold my hand.
       And you don't let go.
       And then we can.

HIM   Listen for the cuckoo come in April
So my mum can write her letter to The Times.

HER   March.

HIM   Or mebbe May.

HER   We sit
at dusk
in the garden
waiting
and listening.

HIM   For one month.

HER   Two months.

HIM   It doesn't sing when it's in Africa.
Only here.

HER   One year. Two years.

HIM   This year, it doesn't come back.

HER   Or this year.

HIM   This year, we don't bother listening out.

HIM   This time –

HER   it's kind of an accident

HIM   they're even standing next to each other.

HER   I'm waiting for my friend.

HIM   Me too.

        –

HER   Who?

HIM   Duncan and James.

HER   Lucy.

        –

        What you going to do?

HIM   Probably hang out in the graveyard.

HER   Gross.
        We're gonna go back to mine.
        Probably watch some films.
        Lucy's bringing an eighteen.

HIM   Wow. You're so fucking hardcore.

HER   Whatever. Yeah, well I
        fucking
        am, actually.

        –

HIM   I've got fags.

HER   Really?

HIM   Yeah. Course.

        –

HER   Do you smoke then?

HIM   No, I just carry fags around wi' me.

        –

HER   When they getting here?

        –

HIM   Tonight
        some time, dunno.

        –

        Why you even hanging around?

HER   We're not at school.

HIM   Get away home I don't want you.

HER   As if I want to be seen wi' you
        when Lucy gets here.

        –

HIM   That's James and Duncan.

HER   Don't worry I'm off.

HIM   Look. Don't be a
        don't be a tit about it.
        They'll be leaving.
        Won't they.
        Before like mouse derby and that kicks off.
        So from like
        you know nine-ish
        I'll be about.

HER   Mebbe I'll be about.
        If Lucy's been picked up.

HIM   Alright.

HER   Alright.

HER   The mobile library comes every week.
We're really lucky.
I leg it out soon as it pulls up in the square.
Howl's Moving Castle.
I take it out every other Wednesday for six months.
It's about

HIM   My mum gets veg and fish from vans.

HER   Today the mobile library
It just doesn't come.

HIM   We have to drive out to town to go to the big Tesco now.
It's great cos they've got Cheetos there for my packed
lunch.

HER   I have to go to the actual library
some Wednesdays
in school holidays
when someone can be bothered to drive me.

HIM   This time –
HER   he's got a cigarette in hand.
HIM   She doesn't.

HER   What you got?
       I do Marlboro.
       Gold.

HIM   –

HER   And the menthol ones cos
       you know
       cancer.

       Beat.

       Ent seen you round much.

HIM   Yeah, well. You're always at school and that.

HER   Yeah.
       So
       What does your mum think about it?

HIM   'Bout what?

HER   You, you know
       like
       dropping out and that.

HIM   Didn't 'drop out' just didn't go back.

HER   Yeah.
       Cool.
       I think I might not. Too. After exams.

       He laughs.

       What?

       Shakes his head.

       Yeah. I reckon I'll probably
       like
       Get a job.

HIM   Yeah? Doing what?

HER –
   Not decided yet.

HIM What the fuck would you do if you left school?

HER You got a job, and I'm cleverer than you are.

HIM You want to come to farm?

HER –
   Can I have one of those?

   He passes her a fag.

   Got a light?

   He sniggers. Lights it.

   Maybe I'll be a secretary. At where my mum works.

   She tries to smoke. With panache.

   How's it then?
   Working life?

HIM Dunno.

HER How's it working for Uncle Harry?

HIM Dunno.

HER You see Adam much?

HIM Course. We do the milking.

HER I used to like
   fucking love
   milking the cows.

HIM We've got machines. They ent pets.

HER Yeah, right. I know.

HIM Fucking big machines as'd might take your hand off if
   you tried.
   Like giant fucking
   Huge, massive, they are.

HER So they're big are they?

HIM Got these big like
   Saucers. Suction things. Stick 'em on udders and
   that's it.

HER   Uncle Harry says the love's gone out of it. Government
           sucked the joy out of farming. He says
           Should be like a family.
           Cattle herd. And can't be like that any more. Not with
           dairy prices the way they are.

HIM   Alright, Tony Blair.

HER   –
           You know he's not Prime Minister any more?

HIM   What d'you know about it anyway?

HER   I mean I know it's not him is in charge now.

HIM   I meant 'bout farm.
           'Bout leaving school and growing up
           actually making money.
           –
           You don't know nothing about owt.

HER   Alright.

HIM   As if your mum'd even let you quit school.

HER   As if she could even stop / me

HIM   Give over. She was off bragging to mine last month
           In our kitchen
           Chatting about how you was 'gifted and talented' or
           some shit like that.

HER   –
           It's not that I'm not that like
           It's just the name of like
           this course.
           This course school are sending me on.
           For kids from local schools who've done really well and
           –
           I didn't apply or anything. It was the teachers.
           I don't think I am.

HIM   You're going to do sixth form.
           Don't be a tit.

           Silence.

HER   It's weird not having you at school.
        Weird not
        like
        picking you up and dropping you off.

HIM   What? Drink and a biscuit?
        Give over.

HER   It's just weird. Cos now it's like
        hardly see you.

        Beat.

HIM   You wanting another?

        He passes her a fag. Lights it.

        What's new wi' you then?

HER   –

HIM   So I work now.
        Operate machinery. Heavy machinery.
        Drive a tractor.
        Noticed my new muscles, have you?

        She sort of laughs.

        What d'you want off of me?

HER   What?

        –

HIM   I need a piss.
        Had one too many
        probably.
        But you know. Feast, in't it.
        –
        What? You gonna watch?

HER   What? It's not like I ent seen it before.

        He laughs.
        He turns. Unzips.

HIM   When did I get to be a grown-up?
        Farmer?

Drinking beer?

–

Know what gets me? I never got me summer holiday.
All of a sudden and it's just like over. Stop school, and
then – can't be not at school, and not working, and you
know
I'd never really thought about that.
Now I'm up at six. Every day.
Be earlier when lambing starts.

HER   I missed you. Over summer.

–

HIM   Why d'you follow me out here?
You don't smoke.
As if.
Your Harry'd cane you.
And you just blow it right out. Been watching you try
and you think you're
trying to be all Hollywood movie and
What you trying on wi' me?
Coming out here after me and wanting to talk about
getting picked up from school together?
Honest?
I reckon you're after something.

HER   I'm not.

HIM   Nah?

–

You're such a kid.

HER   I'm one year younger.

HIM   You're hundred million years younger.

HER   You're an idiot.

HIM   Fuck off then.
If you think I'm such an idiot.

–

Come on, then.
Come on.

He stands too close.
They end up kissing.

I've done it before. With someone else.

HER   Me too. I've done it. Course I have.

They kiss again.

HER   Feast Weekend is like the peak on our horizon.
         Thursday night
         bolts drawn on the gates
         and we're all here.
         All just a load of people sitting down to meat-and-
         two-veg
         in vague hours
         before the slow descent into inebriation.
         Learning each another again.
         Finding our feet among the rabble.

HIM   Feels like the village has its walls up.
         Like a fucking
         battalion
         like – us against the world.

HER   It's pagan
         and ancient
         and none of us remember
         or really kind of care cos
         Tradition's just ours. And it used to be a fertility
         festival but it's just
         Ours. Now.

HIM   They start sponsoring stuff.
         Putting up stalls and
         signs.
         'Parking this way.'

HER   It's mostly for charity, now.
         Run raffles. Charge entry for a road race.
         Raise loads of money.

HIM   Come night though and it's still the same.
         Cover of darkness and day-trippers gone home.
         Lock us in and fill us up.

HER   This time –

HIM   she's in her room.

HER   He's at the window.

HIM   You got a minute?

HER   What you doing!

HIM   Yeah
       Sorry
       sorry.

HER   I might not've had any knickers on!
       You can't just pop up at a girl's bedroom window you
       know.

HIM   You live in a bungalow.

       Beat.

       What you
       ?

HER   We're off out in Scarborough. After.

HIM   ?

HER   Cos it's easier
       on a weekend
       for girls to get in, at this one place.

HIM   Cos you act like a slut.

HER   What?

HIM   You just act like a slut and they let you in? Even
       though you're underage and that?

HER   I'm sixteen.

HIM   Put all
       on your face and batter your eyelashes.

HER   Batter?? What am I a fish?

HIM   Whatever.

HER What's up wi' you?

HIM I just
just don't think it's okay for
girls like you, putting on
all that, and that
and then acting all shocked when you get paid attention
or some lad's grabbed your arse
or raped.
And that.

HER Wow.

HIM What?

HER I didn't realise you were

HIM What?

HER A fuck-off massive dickhead from like the nineteen-fucking-fifties.

HIM I'm right. You know I am.

HER Yeah. Course you are.

HIM Don't you
don't you speak to me like that.

HER Fucking hell. DAD.
What's your problem tonight? Showing up at my window
Saying I deserve to get raped?!

HIM I never said that.

HER Times like these, you know, when I wish I carried around a little recording-device thingy in my pocket cos you don't half come out with some absolute bollocking shite and then pretend you never did.

HIM I'd never want you to get raped.

HER I should fucking hope not!

HIM I'd kill him.
I'd bloody
fucking

throttle him.
Wi' my bare hands.

HER   What are you
        ?

HIM   I would. I'd gut him.
        Like I could do a pig.
        With a butcher's knife.
        Hang him on a
        fucking
        one of them hooks on ceiling
        what they hang cows on down abattoir.
        Through his balls.
        And he'd be bleeding out all over floor.

        Silence.

HER   Are you
        okay?

HIM   Don't you dare say to me that I don't give a
        Cos that's what I'd do.

        Beat.

HER   Thank you
        ?

HIM   S'alright.

        –

HER   Why are you even here?
        We're supposed to be meeting at the pub. And you're

HIM   Oh yeah
        Yeah I don't fancy pub tonight

HER   What??
        But
        it's Feast.

HIM   Yeah. I know.
        But like
        my mum's left and it'll be all over village by tonight.

HER   What?

HIM   She's been
        wi' this
        –

HER   Fuck.

HIM   You know she was doing them salsa classes out in
        town on a Thursday night?

HER   Fuck. She wasn't doing salsa?

HIM   Yeah. No.
        She was going.

HER   Shit.

HIM   She said to m'dad
        in our kitchen, just now
        that he wasn't enough for her and that she had
        dreams and
        fantasies?

HER   Shit.
        You okay?

HIM   I just hate foreign blokes, you know?
        Putting stupid

HER   It's just such a fucking cliché, isn't it?

HIM   What is?

HER   Running off with some Spanish sex god.

HIM   He ent Spanish.

HER   But you said salsa.

HIM   He's called Amit or something, from fucking Bradford
        by way of who-gives-a-fuck.

HER   It's really
        just
        fucked.
        –

        So do you want to stay in tonight?

HIM   Kind've just
        wanna like
        go and sit in barn.

Wi' you.
You know?

–

When I heard them screaming bloody murder at each
other
I listened for a bit
Sitting on stairs like some fucking
And then I just thought –
I thought
I've never once heard him say something like
I've never really actually seen him kiss her or owt.
And all these films and shit with that guy all you lot love
when they're in bed and old and die

HER   Are you talking about Ryan Gosling?

HIM   after that one we watched together and you were
saying all that stuff

HER   But it is just a film.

HIM   But wait a minute.
Like saying about respect and feeling
cherished
was it you said?

HER   Was it?

HIM   Yeah.
Cherished.
And she used that word too.
My mum.

–

And so I thought it'd probably be better to come
round. Better than sitting there on stair and crying
like a
I just wanted to come over here and say that
I sort of cherish you.
Or that I want to.
And now it sounds really fucking stupid.

HER   Shall we just

–

There's some cans in the fridge, I saw.
Mum won't notice.
–

It is Feast, after all.
We don't have to go to the pub.
I can stay here, with you.
If you like.

HER   The English honey bee is endangered.
        I used to see them in the garden all the time.
        Gentle, docile, little things.
        Sandy-coloured, delicate wings.
        You can pick them up and they wouldn't ever sting
        you.
        Let 'em out the window.
        Watch em fly away.
        Tiny little speck in the wind
        off to do some good.

HIM   A swarm of bees fly down our chimney.
        Ten thousand or more.
        I help my dad build a fire and
        I get stung a few times but
        Smoke 'em out. That's the trick.
        Or they'll settle, build a hive. Never get 'em out.
        But the sound of it. Them burning.
        It sounds like
        tornado. A whole fucking army of jets.
        The loudest
        the angriest
        the scariest I ever heard in my life.

HER   This time –

HIM   she finds him in the yard.

HER   He doesn't see her coming.

HER   What you doing here?

HIM   –

Working. It's Monday.

HER   Yeah. Course.

HIM   Where else'd I be?

HER   I just I thought
You know I'm off, right? Today.

–

Should see the Micra. Harry's got all suitcases
strapped to top.
Looks ridiculous.

HIM   Never know how much crap you have till you pack it up.

HER   Not all of it.

HIM   Clothes.

HER   I'm leaving a lot here.
Most of my stuff'll still be here.

–

You not gonna come say bye?

HIM   Said bye last night.

HER   Wasn't really a proper goodbye was it.

HIM   Seemed pretty proper to me.

HER   Thought you might want to
you know.
Wave me off.

HIM   Not really my style is it.

HER   –

I'm coming back next month you know.
And then Christmas not that far.

HIM   Yeah.

HER   You can come visit.

HIM   –
        Yeah.

HER   I'll help with trains.

HIM   What?

HER   Just
        you know.
        Student loan.

HIM   I can manage a train fare.

HER   Didn't say you couldn't.

HIM   Just London I'm not that fussed about.

HER   Yeah I know you're not. But
        I'll be there.

        –

        I'm gonna
        Miss you, you know.

HIM   It's not forever is it. Like you say you're back in three
        weeks
        And then there's Christmas and then three years you're
        back here for good. I'm not
        like
        I'm not worried or owt.

HER   Yeah. Me too.
        I'm not worried.

        –

HIM   Piss him off if you keep him waiting.

HER   Yeah. The Micra's all loaded up. Looks ridiculous.

HIM   Yeah you said.

        –

        I can come by.

Wave.
If you like.

HER   Don't worry. I just
       Didn't know if you'd forgot.

HIM   Course I've not forgot.

       –

HER   Alright. I'll um
       Be seeing you.

HIM   Three weeks.

HER   Yeah. In three weeks.

HIM   At Feast
in evenings
cos it's still light this time of year
all the men play at quoits.
Clay mounds, opposite, wi' spike coming out each.
Throwing like
metal rings, one end t'other.
Makes this sound like

–

Hear it every year late into the night but
not all the men play it.
Just old ones now.
And I don't know it.
And one year it's just not here.
Cos someone's died and no one else knows to set it up.
And it just never comes back.
And I never hear that sound since
that really like
that dull sound or chink of metal near striking metal
and thud of it in clay.
I never hear that sound again
whole rest of my life.

HIM   This time –

HER   he's in a smart suit
buttonhole and all.

HIM   She's in a nice dress.
Not a wedding dress.

HER   Shouldn't you
?

HIM   Got a bit

HER   Yeah. It's quite hot in there.

–

You look good. Scrub up well. Nice suit.

HIM   Cheers. And you.

HER   Third wedding in two months. Going to have to buy
a new one soon.
Mum did say it would start happening all of a sudden.
Wedding season.

–

Lucy looked gorgeous. Really, really

HIM   Yeah.

HER   Must've cost a fortune.

HIM   Wouldn't know. Her dad was paying wont he.

HER   Well, she looks beautiful.

–

Yeah, I got in a bit late.
Missed the aisle bit. I feel really bad
about that.

HIM   Yeah I know.

HER   Oh God. You didn't notice, did you?? I tried to be
quiet. But that
that fucking creaky door.
I just slipped into a side seat though. But it was still

a good view.
I could still see everything.
Lots of flowers, though. Almost got in the
But I kind of just leant, a bit, the whole way through.
And then it was fine.

HIM   Yeah. Could see.

HER   Was I really loud?
Fuck. That's really embarrassing. Can't believe I'm
that girl.

HIM   What girl?

HER   Late to a wedding. What a dickhead.

HIM   Yeah.

HER   Nice buttonhole.

HIM   It's lilac.
You always hated pastels.

HER   –
Pastels??

HIM   Wedding.
Know all about colours now, me.

HER   I would never have thought I'd ever hear you use the
word pastels
in an actual sentence.

HIM   Well I wish I didn't know what it was.
Tell you that. For free.

HER   Yeah, yeah.
God, yeah. Fucking. Pastels.
Weddings.
It's my third, you know, in two months.

HIM   Going to have to get yourself a new party dress at
this rate.

HER   Oh, yeah.
Do you not like it?

HIM   It's fine.

HER   I thought I should
        All the invitations came through the door within the
        space of like
        and so I went out shopping and I was like
        Woman On A Mission. All the birds with one stone,
        I thought.
        Better spend a lot of money on one dress than buy
        a load of cheap ones.

HIM   Or you could buy one cheap one.

HER   Right. But yeah. I spent about hundred and twenty.
        On this.

HIM   How much??

HER   In the sales.
        –
        How's Adam been then?

HIM   Yeah, alright. I mean
        just mostly letting it go over his head.

HER   Probably the best way.

HIM   She's expecting.

HER   Is she??

HIM   Early days.

HER   But she's
        she was, you know
        she was knocking them back, in there.

HIM   You can have a bit. Just a few.
        Our mums did. Didn't do us any harm. People are just
        you know
        scared of shadows, these days.
        And it is her bloody wedding.

HER   Yeah. I mean
        actually I think it isn't such a good idea. Is what they
        say now, about it. Especially during the early days.

HIM   Didn't realise you were a fucking doctor.
        All I'm saying is it's probably the hormones.

HER   Never said I was a doctor but it's just obvious. You're
           meant to be taking the supplements even from the / first

HIM   Alright what are you trying to get pregnant or
           something?

           She laughs.

HER   No.

           –

HIM   She made me shave.

HER   I didn't realise you had a beard.

HIM   It wont Gandalf or owt.

HER   I don't reckon you'd look good with a beard.

HIM   Jen likes it.

           –
           –

HER   So she's
           Lucy
           been a bit of a Bridezilla then?
           I never thought
           you know, never would've thought she'd be that bad.

HIM   As if. Something happens wi' you lot wi' weddings.

HER   ?

HIM   Women.

HER   Yeah. I dunno.
           I mean. I think it probably has something to do with
           the, you know
           probably quite a big deal. Saying you're going to
           spend the entire of the rest of your life with one
           person. And that
           you know
           Saying you're going to love them more than anyone
           else ever
           for the rest of your life.
           And that you love that person you're marrying more
           than anyone else

> that you've ever loved.
> I mean I wouldn't know. But
> probably has something to do with that.

HIM   I don't think it's that.

HER   I mean no you're right there's also like loads of
       cultural signifiers tied up in there. Sociological sort of /
       stuff.

HIM   I reckon it's more to do wi' wanting to dress up like
       a fucking fairy.

       –

HER   Well yeah.
       There's that.

       Music
       Something fairly cheesy.

       What the fuck is
       ?

HIM   First dance.

HER   Oh, God.

HIM   Her choice.

HER   You should probably
       Best man, and that.

HIM   Nah.
       But feel free

HER   No I'll
       I thought you were meant to
       ?

HIM   What?

HER   Isn't the best man meant to dance with the head
       bridesmaid though?

HIM   This bit's just for the bride and groom.

HER   Yeah. Course. I'm being stupid.

HIM   You should know. In't it your third in two months.

HER   Yeah but
        mostly too drunk by this point.

HIM   Hardcore.

HER   That's me.

        –

        It's a shit song.

HIM   Fucking awful.

        –

HER   Do you want to
        ?

HIM   ?

HER   Was just thinking
        just running through all the times
        like in my head like a slideshow and
        I don't think that we have ever
        I mean we've done most everything together me and
        you, but I don't think that we have ever actually had
        a dance. Together.
        –
        Shall we?
        Just, you know
        for fun. And that.

HIM   If you want.

HER   Okay.

HIM   Not inside.
        Here.

HER   Alright.

        They dance. Sort of.

        You're not
        not bad

HIM   I have done this before.

HER   Course you have. Me too.

        –

        –

        I miss you.

        –

        Should I leave you alone?
        I feel like I should leave you alone.
        God. I should just fuck off, shouldn't I?
        I should just like
        just
        fuck right off.
        Why don't you tell me?
        Go on. Please. Go on, please just tell me to fuck off.

HIM   Why?
        We're having a nice dance.

HER   Don't. Don't don't don't.

HIM   What?

HER   I don't want to
        I'm not an overdramatic sort of person.

HIM   Yeah you are.

HER   I'm not
        sentimental.

HIM   Are you not?

HER   Doesn't your chest hurt?
        Feel like my gullet

HIM   Gullet?

HER   My gullet. My windpipe. Like my
        my
        my breastbone. Feels tight.
        Like I can't and I just don't know how to

        –

I wish you
I wish you weren't so
like, stoical.

HIM   –
Sorry.

HER   Or just like
upright. And just
certain.

HIM   Alright.

HER   I feel fucked up.

HIM   I'm sorry you feel like that.

HER   Oh, fuck off.

HIM   What now?

HER   I'm going in.

HIM   Okay.

HER   No.
Stop me.

HIM   Why?

HER   Fuck's sake.

HIM   You going in or what?

HER   –
I don't want to leave.
I don't want you to go in.

HIM   Never said I was going in.

HER   I'm going to stay out here for a bit.
–
Aren't you scared of being caught out here?
With me?
All this time?

HIM   –

HER   Let's just sit here for a little bit and
        and then I'll probably feel a lot better after that.
        Could you hold my hand please?
        Could I
        would you mind if I put my head on your shoulder?
        Please could you put your arm round me?
        Like that.
        Yes.
        Just for a bit.
        I'll just stay out here, for a while, with you.

HER That one's the Wilson house.
   Cross the beck –
   Pattinsons live there.
   Then there's Thompsons, Banks, Holland round the
   square.
   That white house is the Smith house.
   That nice one.
   More Thompsons behind the church.
   Up the lane back there's Nichols.

HIM That one was the Wilson house.
   Cross the beck –
   don't know who lives there.
   Then there's Thompsons, dunno, dunno.
   Houses round the square mostly holiday homes now.
   That white house is a B&B.
   That nice one. The Smiths died.
   House behind the church is only used on weekends.
   I've never met 'em.
   They don't come to pub.
   Up the lane back there's Nichols
   but it's up for sale
   but they can't shift it cos it's listed and no one wants it
   wi'out planning permission to extend.

HIM   This time –
HER   he's got a pint in hand, still in his overalls.
HIM   She's still got her car keys in hand.

HIM   I've only got a half-hour.

HER   I should go up soon anyway.

HIM   Got darts at six.
        You ent been home yet?

HER   Not yet. Thought I'd
        Was driving past, and you know
        Saw your house – first on the corner.
        Just pulled over, before I knew it.
        Turned the wheel and
        Didn't realise you'd still be working.

HIM   Adam and Harry's back there.

HER   Where?

HIM   At table round the corner. You want to say hello?

HER   Has he seen me?

HIM   Just having a pint. Obviously we've finished for the day.
        Has who seen you?

HER   Uncle Harry.

HIM   Well, yeah.

HER   What?

HIM   That car of yours. Hard to miss.

HER   It's good in the city.
        Got really good fuel economy for city driving.
        How is he, then?

HIM   Harry?

HER   Yeah.

HIM   Fine.

HER   Shall we just
        You want to duck into yours?

HIM   I'm alright here. I'll finish my drink.

HER   How've you been?

        He laughs.

        Don't laugh at me.

HIM   What you doing back? It's not Christmas.

HER   No. I just
        Thought I'd visit.

        He laughs again.

        What?

        –

        You haven't said. How you are.

HIM   I'm good me.

HER   Always good.
        Any news?

        –

        Anything new to report?

HIM   Like what?

HER   Just – you know. General life question.
        Everything's fine with me, too. Great. I got a new flat.
        Moved in a couple of weeks ago. It's a bit
        But it's in a nicer area. I live right round the corner from
        this arthouse cinema. It's nice – snazzy. I don't see the
        but they've got a lovely bar. Good nachos. You know?
        Are you finished? Look, shall we head back to yours,
        for a bit?

HIM   Why?

HER   It's a bit
        loud.

HIM   There's no one in here.

        Beat.

        So what you doing wi' yourself?

HER   I'm the administrator for a start-up, right now. I mean it's not exactly
         but you know. Got to start somewhere.

HIM   Sounds fancy.

HER   Do you even know what an administrator does?

HIM   Alright.

HER   And what are you doing with yourself these days?

HIM   Still on farm, aren't I.

         She laughs.

HER   Of course.

HIM   Don't laugh at me.

HER   I'm not.

HIM   You just did.

HER   It wasn't at you.

HIM   You always do. That fucking annoying little laugh of yours. That ent changed.

HER   Don't be / so

HIM   Patronising.

HER   Don't be so loud.

HIM   You embarrassed?

HER   –

HIM   Rum and Coke for you? Spiced? Just like always?

HER   Stella for you. Just like always.

HIM   Alright. You drink it too.

HER   Aged fourteen in barns. Think I'm past it.

HIM   See, this is the difference
         between me and you. I'm not
         About liking Stella.
         About still drinking Stella, even now.

About really liking it still, and not going off and deciding
Deciding to like champagne even / more instead

HER   I don't like champagne

HIM   Just because you / think

HER   Gives me a headache.

HIM   Just because you're there, deciding. Being like –
I shouldn't like Stella any more. Fourteen, nicked cans,
chugged in the haystacks. In that sort of voice, like
You're like – nah, shouldn't any more.
Shouldn't.

Silence.

So how's that boyfriend of yours? Been a while since
he was up visiting.

HER   We're not together any more.

HIM   Why's that then?

HER   Nothing in particular.

HIM   Odd reason to split up.

HER   Break up. You make it sound like we were married.

HIM   Why'd you split up for no reason?

HER   It wasn't for no reason.

HIM   You hear Emma get married?

HER   Of course.

HIM   It's all going on up here. Marriages. Babies.

HER   Yeah. Half the kids from our year knocked up by
eighteen. Great.

HIM   Wasn't just 'knocked up'.

HER   It's different down south.

HIM   Just people deciding to have kids.

HER   Kids deciding to have kids.

HIM   You've got it all figured out, haven't you.

HER   We do it all later.

HIM   We? 'City folk'?
         Enlightened?

HER   Big word.

HIM   Patronising bitch.

HER   Stop being so loud!

HIM   You embarrassed?

HER   –

HIM   What you embarrassed for?

HER   Stop it. Harry's just round the corner. They'll be
         listening in. You know they will. Be halfway round the
         village by teatime.

HIM   –
         He's not round the corner.

HER   But you said

HIM   Wanted to see if you were still embarrassed to be out
         wi' me.

HER   –
         I'm sorry. I didn't mean to sound like
         Didn't mean to have a go.

HIM   I've seen it. You and him – your lad – up here, at
         Christmas time. Never looking in each other's eyes.
         Too busy looking over your shoulders.

HER   Over my shoulder?

HIM   No. Not behind. The other way. Over the other
         person's shoulder.

HER   Right.

HIM   Not that you're looking backwards.
         That you're looking for the next thing. Next best thing.
         For just in case it comes along.
         You know, I always knew you'd end up out of here.

HER   Yeah?

HIM   It's not a compliment. You've always had those
wandering eyes, like. Looking over my shoulder.

HER   –
Why are you so keen to talk about this? Marriage and
babies and all that.

HIM   You started it.

HER   But you have an opinion. You would never have been
bothered before.
Would've just laughed me off.

–

You're getting married, I heard.
I thought you might
want to tell me.

HIM   You don't change.

HER   I do.

HIM   No you don't.

HER   It's just that
–
I do.
Actually. I do.
–
It's just every time I come back
here
and you all just expect me to slot back in but I'm
you know
I'm different.
Like
bigger.
You know those toys babies play with? Those shapes?
A triangle they try and slam into a square hole?

HIM   –

HER   But somehow
Somehow I get sanded down. And then
I wonder

how I'd ever thought I'd changed to begin with.
–
I thought I'd come here and

HIM   What?
       Go on then.

He doesn't make a move, and neither does she.

HER   I love the way the road looks
        on the way in.
        That sort of curve like
        like a mum's belly.
        Everything's kind of hidden
        until
        And when I come round that curve
        my breath and my muscles and every inch of me
        It's sort of just like
        my whole body has this
        huge
        sigh. Like
        all my organs settling into place.

HIM   Bloody death trap.
        Amount of accidents happen on that corner.
        Fucking day-trippers.
        They've put
        I got points.
        On my licence.
        For speeding.
        In my own
        On my road.
        –

        In a fucking tractor.

HER   This time –
HIM   he's at her front door
HER   attempts a bit of a carol.

HIM   Come on then I'm freezing my bollocks off here.

HER   But I was enjoying that.

HIM   Give over.

        –

        Where's your folks?

HER   Must be out. I only got here like

HIM   Yeah I know I saw the car on the way in.
        Pub?

HER   Bit late. Long drive.

HIM   Alright then, we'll do it Boxing Day.

HER   I'm leaving early 26th.

HIM   That soon?

        –

        Alright then. Tomorrow.
        You hear about my dad being badly?

HER   I should've sent flowers or something.

HIM   No rush he ent dead yet.

HER   Mum said he's to moved to a um

HIM   Yeah. When he started shitting the bed
        you know
        clear up enough of that every day without having to
        deal wi' his.

HER   He'll be more comfortable there I'm sure.

HIM   I mean he fucking hates it.
        Fucking hates me for putting him in there but you know
        Actually costs a bomb. Not that he's grateful.

HER   It must be really hard for you.

HIM   It is, yeah.
       It is really hard.
       Thanks.

       –

HER   So

HIM   –
       What?

HER   We going to talk about this then? As you're here.

HIM   Alright.
       Yeah, alright.

HER   –
       Look I don't know if
       I don't know if maybe you just want to talk it all
       through with me.
       Like, everything that's gone down till this point cos like
       I mean obviously I haven't been here
       and I do acknowledge that it's not just my opinion that
       matters.

HIM   Alright.
       I mean it matters just as much as mine.

HER   As he says
       I did 'fuck off'. Didn't I.

HIM   What?

HER   You know it hurts when he says stuff like that.
       Harry.

HIM   Right.
       I mean
       you been talking to him about this have you?

HER   Course.

HIM   Right.
       I mean
       that does put me in a bit of an awkward
       Why go talking to Harry before you talk to me?

HER   Cos it's his
       What?

HIM   –
       What we talking 'bout here?

HER   We're talking about the barns he wants converting into
       a fucking hotel. Yeah?

HIM   –
       Yeah. Course.

HER   You alright? You look a bit

HIM   Nah I'm
       Sorry what we
       ?
       Sorry.
       What we talking about here?

HER   Harry.
       It's about us
       Fucking
       Saving him from himself.
       –
       Like a petition. Or something.

HIM   –

HER   This place is special, right? I've never come across
       anywhere else like it. Not anywhere
       in the whole world.
       I've read hundreds of books and I've never read of
       anywhere like it.

HIM   I don't read books.

HER   I mean let me just
       look, it's smack bang in the middle of the village right?
       So you can't just think about the thing itself. This
       stupid, commercial
       You have to think about like
       what about a car park? Where's people going to park
       their cars?

HIM   I dunno. Side of the road like everyone else does?

HER   What about the farm?

HIM   What d'ya mean?

HER   Like
        Those outbuildings are being fucking used.

HIM   Yeah but
        selling cattle herd. Aren't we.

HER   Are you?

HIM   Changing to pigs cos
        You know. Dairy's fucked. And
        can't fuck bacon, can you?

HER   Right.
        So the answer's getting rid of a six-generation cattle
        herd is it?

HIM   Mind you
        Tories drink milk too
         so probably won't stop 'em.

HER   What?

HIM   Fucking bacon.

HER   –
        I thought you'd be on my side.

HIM   I always
        like I am but
        You know.
        Thought about my job if farm goes under and
        –
        Shoulda bought your milk locally, shouldn't you.

HER   What's that supposed to mean?

HIM   Don't get angry wi' me.
        Look no wonder you've got his back up. All this and
        You wanting to be going round village talking to
        people about his business?
        You're like meant to be his
        –
        D'you know I'm having to sell my dad's house.

HER   What? Why?

HIM   Cos it needs re-rendering and there's damp and no
        central heating sorted even. Needs some proper money
        putting in it.
        And I don't have it. For it or for
        To spend for
        you know
        for looking after him.

HER   You could do it yourself though.

HIM   Mebbe I could. But d'you know there's this contractor
        or
        estate agent or something. Been putting letters through
        all the doors in the village. Says he represents clients
        looking for 'quality properties with character and
        privacy, in this desirable location'.
        And do you know how much they're offering?
        Through the nose.

HER   You haven't spoken to him?

HIM   They came round to have a look, and it was like they
        were seeing something different I couldn't even see
        right in front of me.
        We'll put a garden room here, and extend over there,
        and ooooh how very dated and d'you know
        it made me a bit embarrassed, to be standing there,
        listening to them, hearing them talk about this house
        like I'd
        Let it down.
        –

        What I'm saying is stuff's already changing.
        Cos name me one person moved here when we were
        kids.
        –

        They were talking about putting a stable in the garden.
        For horses.
        I'm like – what the fuck are you wanting a horse for in
        your garden?

HER   You don't have to sell it.
        This is what I mean – you and Harry it's like you're

just wanting to throw money at the situation rather
than actually work at it.

Think about it, if you did that house up together, you
and Jen – how meaningful that would be. Raising your
kids there.

HIM   Jen?

HER   When you're married.

HIM   Jen's not
        Jen's back home. With her mum.

        –

HER   I hadn't heard.

        –

        I'm sorry. That's rubbish. She was lovely, Jen.

HIM   Was she?

HER   Yeah. I always thought she was a really lovely girl.
        I always said that.

        –

HIM   So you were just
        ?

HER   What?

HIM   I'm just a bit

HER   You should go online.

HIM   What?

HER   You should
        you know. Is there someone? Anyone new on the
        horizon? I mean
        I only did because my friend Zoe – she's a friend from
        work.
        She bullied me into signing up with her because she
        didn't want to do it by herself, and so I did, but like,
        mostly just taking the piss. But it's crazy because
        that's how I met Spencer.

So I mean, just you never know how or why these
things work out.

HIM   –

HER   So maybe things happen for a / reason.

HIM   When was that?

HER   Just, only a few months ago. He's a
He's not what you'd expect for me, I think.
That's what everyone keeps saying because he's just so
together and
Grown Up.
Mum's fucking thrilled. Cos he's a lawyer.

HIM   Your mum is, is she.

HER   They got on really well. Which is obviously a bit
you know, a bit disconcerting. For me.

She laughs.

–

He made me a spreadsheet.
I mean – just – that's why my mum's all
Cos he's just like really focused and motivated.
He asked me what I wanted to do with my life and
I was just like, at first, I was like – I have no fucking
idea. Actually, I change my mind every few minutes.
All the time.

HIM   Yeah. As you do.

–

So what was it you wanted off me this time?

HER   –
What?

HIM   'Bout Harry's plans. Is that what you're wanting?
Shall I go off and have a go at him for you?
Get myself the sack, shall I? Over this barn of yours?

HER   No I
I just wanted to
talk to you.

But you know it's the right thing to do. And we
us
we have a responsibility.

HIM   Well I ent doing what you want.

HER   It's literally just a fucking signature on a fucking
computer.

HIM   D'you know, it might come as a surprise to you
but there are people that actually live here. In this
village.

HER   I'm aware.

HIM   We don't all come and go as we bloody well please.
I know you want to keep it frozen in time like your
own little snow globe.

HER   What are you talking about?

HIM   Girl I knew
she woulda used to get what I'm saying.
You can't just get everything you want. You have to
just decide, sometimes, what you want. Where you're
gonna be.
Mebbe that lawyer of yours knows you best after all cos
Girl I knew
she woulda known this in't a museum.
This is a working village, and I work here, and I live
here, and don't you dare come to me and tell me what
to do.
Cos if you want to buy your fucking nut milk from
Tesco then mebbe we have to shovel pig shit instead.
Or you'll be taking our farms and you'll mek 'em into
very little pretty little houses like of only your lad can
afford.

HER   You think that just because you still exist here every
day that no one else can have an opinion?
This is my home too.

HIM   I'll listen to opinions, just not yours.
And d'you know
do you even think for a second? Sometimes?

For a really clever little girl as you are you can be
really fucking

–

Course he wants to knock it down and start again what
with everything that's ever happened in that barn to him.
Must be like a fucking
Every time he has to see it. Walk by it. Go in it.
D'you not think that all he sees ghosts?
And you're nagging about your little playground you
don't want to change.

HER   This isn't about William for him this is about money
and you know it.

–

HIM   D'you know, we were trying for a littl'un, me and Jen.
We'd lost one. By accident she was
And then we were trying again.
And d'you know sometimes it'd be your voice ringing
round my head,
telling me are there greater things to be doing in my
life.

–

Fuck you.

HER   I'm sorry for you, that that happened to you.

HIM   Fuck
You.

–

HER   Look I didn't want to have an argument.
I don't want us to keep picking at things like they're
infected scabs that won't heal.

HIM   More like a grave.
Right?
More like a grave that won't stay dug.

–

Am I right?

–

What I'm saying is
feel free to jump in
correct me if I'm wrong
I'm not the one with a fucking PhD here

HER   BA

HIM   but what I'm saying is if we're liking this
and us
to anything
then it'd be a grave. A big, dark, horrible, dirty grave
that won't stay dug.

HIM   Holstein Friesian, two years old
        Shall we start three hundred? Any takers?

HER   Twenty

HIM   Fifty

HER   Eighty

HIM   Going five eighty in a minute five eighty in a minute

HER   Fifty, hundred, fifty, hundred

HIM   Sold.
        That's how it is.
        One by one by one they go.

HIM   This time –

HER   he's working outside.

HIM   Top off.

HER   Careful. I might've been an old lady.
       Give her a heart attack.

       –

       What you doing all the way out here?

HIM   Working.

HER   On a Sunday?

HIM   Not for Harry.

HER   ?

HIM   I bought it off him. In the pub at New Year's he starts
       going on about this patch like it's a waste of space and
       how he's only needing it for the thoroughfare so

HER   Oh.

HIM   How it was only ever you used it, for sledging and the
       like.
       So he wanted rid.

       –

       He was drunk, mind. Probably still angry wi' you.

HER   –
       Congratulations.

HIM   It's a pile of shite as far as farming it goes but you know

HER   So why did you buy it?

HIM   Dunno. Done me a good deal.

HER   I'm sure he did.

       Beat.

HER   So what you planning for it?

HIM   It's useless for crop. But was thinking
           I met this lad out in N'thallerton, market day. From
           down south. One of them with the you know
           with the beards.
           He was selling wool – rare-breed, alpaca and that. And
           the mark-up on his stuff. Was thinking I could get
           some of them out here.

HER   Sounds good.

HIM   Start small but you know
           Feels good. I've never owned owt in my life before.
           Nowt proper.
           And now I can be like – get off my land!
           To be fair. There's no right of way.

           –

HER   It's weird. We used to play here.

HIM   Yep.

HER   You broke your leg sledging into that post.

HIM   Happy times.

HER   And playing dens all in the blackthorn.

HIM   It's a fucking nightmare that is.

HER   You're not clearing it?

HIM   It's a weed. Taking up half the hill.

HER   It's gorgeous in flower.

HIM   Yeah for like one week of the year.

HER   You could harvest the sloes. Make gin and sell it.

HIM   How many hundreds of thousands of sloes do I have to
           pick to make anything on that?

HER   But it's better than nothing.

HIM   For a week of dinky white flowers in spring and gin at
           backend I think I'll do without.

HER   Well
           I guess it's your shout.

HIM   He's left me in a right way with 'em. Thirty years these
things must've been here. I can chainsaw the branches
but the fucking roots are the problem. See how deep
down they go?
And it's not even that they're just deep. They grow
down and then across and then come up again and
it's like
what you think's a completely different plant on surface
– it's all from the same roots. I keep digging down and
hacking away and right when I think I'm done
just keeps on going down deeper.

HER   Probably easier just to let it be then.

HIM   Easier for who?
Nice try.

           –

HER   I saw your dad's house sold.

HIM   Yep.

HER   Was it those
      ?

HIM   Not them, but like.

HER   I noticed the conservatory.

HIM   No horses yet though.

HER   Looks bigger.

HIM   'Tis.

           –

           You want to hear summat funny?

HER   Go on.

HIM   You want to hear where I live now?

HER   Where?

HIM   You remember that little cottage we used to take the
piss out of when we was kids? One the church used to
give Blind Jack for a peppercorn rent?
That's where I live now.

Do you know what they call it? Like, the official name.
It's called the poor house.

HER   –
        That's not funny.

HIM   But you've got to laugh, don't you.

        –

        I wanted to ask you a favour.

HER   What kind of favour?

HIM   I reckon you owe me one.

        –

        I want the farm.

HER   The
        what farm?
        Harry's farm?

HIM   He's got to want to retire soon in't he.
        He dun't want to be eighty and still arguing wi' parish
        council about churning up the verges. And who's he
        got to give it to?
        It's dead sad – what happened to his boy.
        Probably always why he doted on you.

HER   Don't say that. It makes me feel guilty when you say
        that.

HIM   But it's not normal is it? Normally you've got a lad to
        leave it to. Or a nephew or summat but there's no one.
        Or no one I know of.

HER   No, you're right. There's no one.

HIM   And even if there was, you work, don't you. You work
        there and then you get passed it on. Thing like a farm,
        it ent something you just get handed.
        It's something you earn.
        –

        And I know I've not much right and what's so different
        from me than every other lad he's got working for him.

HER   Except for you were the first boy born to the village in
        twenty years.

HIM   Exactly. And even if they move here at six years or six
        months

HER   It's not the same.

HIM   No. It's not the same as us.
        And Harry does appreciate that. He mayn't like me,
        but he knows we're from that same stock.

        –

        These fields got some of my sweat
        some of my blood even
        in them. That'll mean summat to him.

HER   But I can't
        how do I ask him to just give you his farm?

HIM   I don't want him to give it me I just
        I want a chance to take it off him but it'll have to be
        slow.
        And like we did here – we didn't need lawyers or owt.
        I could take it over slowly. He could take a cut of
        profits, till I can pay him back.

        Beat.

HER   I mean
        It's not a small ask.

HIM   I know.

HER   Of me and him.

HIM   If you don't want me to have it

HER   Of course I'd want you to

HIM   Then what?
        After all your rabble-raising
        After all that and sacking off his plans for his
        retirement
        Thought you might be pleased.
        We could see him right. Us two.
        Even after all your

All that.

–

You going to do this one thing I've ever asked off you
or what.

–

HER   Stop making me feel guilty.

HER There's no more space in the graveyard.
     They let just anyone get buried here
     but suddenly it gets like
     Someone actually dies
     who's lived here
     and there's nowhere for them left to go.
     Have you ever heard of that?
     I mean obviously it must happen somewhere but
     –

     They want to be buried next to their son.
     But the plot's been taken by some poet from down
     south
     looking for a picturesque eternity.

HIM Field next to church is the old plague graveyard.
     There's rules about that.

HER And I can walk around and these stones here
     these bits of marble, these new ones.
     I don't recognise a single name.
     –

     There's nowhere left for us to die.

HER   This time –
HIM   they're in black.

HER   I don't want the whole village seeing me cry.

        –

        Get me another will you.
        Can't stand that new landlady.

        –

        What's with these like
        candles in jam jars?
        Fucking
        It wasn't grey before. Was it?

HIM   I don't come here any more.

HER   When did all this happen?

HIM   Past six months or so. Some of the beers she's got
        four-fifty a pint.
        Probably what sent him over the edge.

HER   Probably.

HIM   Hey, it was a joke.

HER   Where've you been? Hardly seen you.

HIM   You've been busy. With the funeral and that.

HER   I've been looking after Auntie Caroline.
        She's been talking about moving out to town. Getting
        one of those new-builds, cos of her arthritis and
        'while she still can'.
        Can you believe that?

HIM   Yeah.

HER   It's only been like a couple of weeks and she's talking
        like that.
        I've only seen her cry once. Over the kettle. And
        I thought – fuck, finally, here's something I can like
        And what she says is – she just can't get used to

boiling the kettle for one. And how much electricity is
that wasting? Boiling the kettle for two all the time
when you only need enough for one?

–

HER   If I had all the money in the world I'd buy this pub and
turn it back into a shithole.
Fucking
I'll give you BISTRO.

HIM   Alright keep it down you.

HER   –
Mum told me off for swearing yesterday.
I only said git.
Said that must've been London taught me that.

Laughs.

Get me another.
Shall we have Stella?

HIM   Seriously?

HER   Old times' sake.
Was it you that found him?

HIM   What?

HER   I heard it was you that found him.

HIM   –

HER   Tell me about it.

HIM   I don't think / you

HER   Tell me.

–

HIM   He'd been out in the lower fields, after lunch.
We'd had sarnies. And me and Adam went off on
tractor and Harry wanted to
I dunno but he wanted to go down there for some
reason or other.

–

Got late. Caro brought us out a brew and
She ant seen him.
Adam had the new littl'un to get back to so I went to see
Not that we actually thought anything was

–

He'd found his way over to a bale and sort of propped
himself up and was just looking around and waiting.
But he looked alright you know.
I did
I did leg it.
But by time I got back he'd just sort of slipped away,
quiet as.
I'd never seen a

–

His eyes were still open, looking up. Sun going down.
Thought it be creepy but his eyes were sort of lit up wi'
it. Was one of those evenings that looks like someone's
taken a pink highlighter pen to the sky. Bit windy,
some cloud cover.
I sat wi' him till someone come.
I could see the clouds going over in the sky but in his
eyes.

–

Let's get them beers in.

–

HER   We're good, yeah?
       Me and you.
       We're good now, yeah?

HIM   What you talking about?

HER   We've been through the mill. Me and you. Haven't we.

HIM   Do you want me to get you some water?

HER   Stop trying to look after me.

–

Sorry it's just
Sorry. It's all just in my head and
I'm finding it hard to look at you right now.

And I've got to say a few words. In a bit.
About my uncle. About my dead uncle.

HIM   Yeah. I know.

HER   And it's a struggle like
even fucking like
Shit.
Everything feels fucking
Like I
you know
Like I did fucking
That.
And then he

HIM   You don't have / to

HER   Shut up I've got a point just
You made me lose my train of thought.

HIM   You alright?

HER   You know I do remember
All of the stuff he
It's not like I never appreciated it.

–

Do you remember
he'd slip me the bus fare to Scarborough?
He would.
On the sly.
Even though I know
I knew

–

I'd be standing there three cans in already.
Swaying.
Fucking
Child.
Remember his eyebrows going up and me just
fucking
sticking my hand out but he didn't
You know he didn't even flinch
At Me.
Just that like –
you know his

that huge – but like, brief – deep, sigh of his.
And it kind of rattled
sorry
kind of
kind of
rumbled in his throat.
–
And three quid in my hand.
–
I thought he'd stopped loving me.
But actually
turns out
he didn't.
–
Stop it.
Don't touch me.
I don't want the whole fucking village seeing me cry.
–
Let's get a drink.

HIM   Probably not the best / idea.

HER   We've got stuff
           we should probably talk about. Because I had Caroline
           like
           My Auntie Caroline she
           We had a sit-down.
           Well all of us. My mum as well.
           And I don't want you to think I'm a bitch for not
           telling you.

HIM   For not telling me what?

HER   So it was about the er
           the you know
           The will. And
           his
           The farm.
           –
           He's um
           he left the farm for me.
           To me.

And at first I was like

–

Shiiiiiiiit.

–

It's not like I'm going to be a farmer.
Well actually I guess I am. Actually.

HIM   You're not like
        being serious?

HER   I am a bit.
        I mean I am.

HIM   He's fucking left you the farm?

HER   Yeah.

HIM   Outright?

HER   I mean there's debts
        obviously.

HIM   Obviously.

HER   You're
        okay?

HIM   I assumed it was fucked. Because we only talked about
        you know, my plan, not so long ago and I reckoned
        you hadn't had chance to have it out wi' him cos he
        hadn't mentioned owt to me
        Sorry I should
        It is a funeral. Sorry. Let's be more
        But he left it to you. Fucking perfect!!

HER   Yeah?

        –

        Why is it perfect?

HIM   –

HER   I can't
        Fuck
        Why are you making this difficult??

HIM   What are you saying?

HER   I can't just

HIM   What about your spreadsheet?

HER   My what?

HIM   Your spreadsheet and London and fucking
        you know like Greenpeace and shit.
        What about all that?

HER   I'm having to rethink.

HIM   That ent rethinking that's a
        fucking three-sixty.

HER   One-eighty.

HIM   Whatever.
        Come on. You going to do over your life at this age?

HER   What age?

HIM   We ent young any more.

HER   I mean we are quite.

HIM   All our like
        people are settled and
        –

        Thought you always wanted to get away from all this.
        –

        What about him
        your lad.

        –

HER   I can't give you the farm.

HIM   You're just upset at the moment.

HER   I can't.

HIM   We'll do the same deal as I'd've done wi' Harry.

HER   He left it to me.

HIM   You ent
        you ent doing this
        to me.

HER   Look I'm
           I didn't expect it.

           –

HIM   Did you not.

HER   But look all those things you said
           about it just being about working and
           you know I give a shit and it's mine now so it's like
           perfect.
           You get to keep your job. It's like a
           Yay.

HIM   Do I now.
           Yay.

HER   Oh fucking stop it with them Yorkshireman questions.
           'Do I now???'

           –
           –

           Say something.
           Look at me don't
           fuck don't just turn your face from me.
           If you're angry then just say that you're angry.
           If you want to hit me then here just hit me.

HIM   I'm not going to fucking hit you.

HER   Fuck. I'm sorry. I'm drunk. I'm sorry.
           But look at us.
           Come on. Look at us.
           But this is basically like
           it'll be what you want actually.
           Cos like
           it's me and you isn't it.
           It's fucking
           Us.
           And I know
           like
           I've been all over the place I know
           and all the time I've been meeting these amazing like
           these people I thought I had all this in common with and

And you – and your Jen – of course.
And after all of that
After all of them
Look – where I am.
I'm back here in this fucking pub with fucking
You.
And that has to like
That means something.
Right?
–

Are you going to say something?

HIM   I'm not going to work for you.

HER   I thought I'd be trapped here
and I am sort of
but you know I've suddenly realised that we're sort of
just trapped wherever we go.

HIM   You owe me that farm.

HER   I do not.

HIM   What the hell have you done to earn it?

HER   I dunno but it just belongs to me doesn't it and us
fighting about it isn't going to do anything!

HIM   Cos blood's thicker than water.

HER   OBVIOUSLY.

HIM   You left.

HER   For fuck's sake
Can you not appreciate that it took some guts moving
away and trying to do something different?
I don't know how you're looking like the hero here,
I really don't.
And
just
NO
You're not entitled to my family's farm
no matter how many paid days you've put in.

And yeah, I KNOW that I'm fucking shouting!
What you so scared of everyone hearing your business
now?
You embarrassed? Am I speaking too fucking loudly?
–

Get off me. I'm trying to speak.
I'm going to make a speech about my dead dad
about my dead uncle.
Hiya, everyone, and thanks for coming.
It really means a lot.

HIM   Stop it.

HER   Don't touch me.

HIM   You're embarrassing yourself.

HER   Wait – where are you going?? Don't you fucking

HIM   What do you want off of me?

HER   –
I'm coming home.

HIM   You always say that.

HER   I've never said that you just like to think it.

HIM   Yeah because I just make everything up in my head
like you coming here and telling me to not marry Jen.

HER   I NEVER FUCKING EVER ONCE SAID YOU
SHOULDN'T MARRY HER.

HIM   You're such
You
Such a fucking

HER   Would you like a dictionary?

HIM   You are a selfish bitch.

HER   Boring, backwards, ignorant, boring

HIM   Wouldn't he just be proud of you.

HER   –

HIM   I'm sure Harry'd be really fucking proud
       looking down at you right now.
       –
       Don't worry, Caroline.
       I'm off.
       I wouldn't stay here
       even if you paid me.

HER   This time –

       This time –

       This time –
       I'm panting

HIM   She's panting.

HER   Heavily.

HIM   As though she's just run a

HER   Hey.
       Hi.
       I was just running past and
       saw someone in here and
       Thought it looked like you.

HIM   What are you doing?

HER   Just five K.

HIM   No I mean here. With this.

HER   Oh right. Yeah.
       It's um
       getting converted. Into a holiday cottage.
       –
       I know it probably looks
       after everything that's happened
       But the plans and everything were already drawn up
       and really we actually
       But we didn't need it, since the dairy herd sold.
       And I had to look through the accounts.
       –
       I do feel like a proper tit about it, if that makes you feel
       any better.
       Can't look some people in the face after all I went on
       about it before.
       But it's not a hotel. It'll just be a little
       something for someone on the weekends.
       And mostly people have just been really supportive,
       of me. Cos it's all just a really steep learning curve.

–

I haven't seen you.

HIM   I ent been here.

HER   I know.

HIM   So that's why you ent seen me.

–

HER   When they started digging up the foundations I found
that
you know that thing you won on the tombola once.
Can't remember what you call it.
You throw it. And it's meant to come back to you.
Only it never worked. I mean probably did really, but
we couldn't do it right.

HIM   Boomerang.

HER   Yeah. That's it.
–
I put it in the garage if you

HIM   Wont it wooden? Must be rotten through.

HER   It isn't. If you want it.
I did go to the trouble of rescuing it.

HIM   Nah I'm alright.

–

HER   I can't think of a way to ask without sounding

HIM   What?

HER   What you doing back?

HIM   –
Dad's house is selling.

HER   I saw the sign.

HIM   I got an appointment to have a look but
you know. Decided I ent gonna bother.

HER   Why not?

HIM   You seen the asking price?

         Beat.

HER   Sorry.

HIM   Not your fault.

         –

HER   Come back to mine. For a cup of tea.
         Caroline'd love to see you.

HIM   Nah.

HER   I did get a telling-off you know, after our
         At the funeral.
         She's not
         upset with you or anything.

         –

         Mum said it would get worse before it gets better.
         Us.
         But she said
         she said that you know
         I can't remember the exact words but it was something
         like
         She says you have people
         you have people and they're either for a reason, a season
         or for life.
         –
         We're not a reason or a season.
         Are we.
         –
         Fuck.
         Why am I
         ?!

HIM   You cry easily.

HER   I do not.

         –

HIM   Do you remember getting me bollocked here?

HER   I know.

HIM   And I'd told you not to go in in the first place and it
        was me got the hiding.

HER   Can I ask
        where are you now?
        Where are you living?

HIM   –
        I'm going to go away for a bit, I reckon.

HER   Where?

HIM   Dunno yet.
        New Zealand mebbe.

HER   New Zealand??

HIM   They've got farms.

HER   Maybe you should start with Kent.

HIM   I've already got a ticket, actually.

HER   But you are coming back
        ?

        –

        Tell you what
        I'll buy your dad's house for you.

        She laughs.
        He doesn't.

        I'm living at the house now.
        The farmhouse.
        Caroline's found a place, out in Thirsk. And I've been
        thinking
        It's a big house to be rattling round in by myself.
        And I'd rather not
        I'd rather not live there alone.
        That's not how I'd imagine it.

HIM   What about your mum.

HER   I don't want to live with my mum.

        –

So what I'm saying to you is
Do you want to?
With me?

–

Would you like to live there, with me.

HIM   I just said to you I'm off to New Zealand.

HER   I know you did.
You can see this as a
grand gesture, if you like.

HIM   Grand?

HER   Ryan Gosling film, if you like.

–

HIM   Sorry.

HER   Don't say sorry.

HIM   I'm sorry.

HER   You don't have to go off just because I did.

HIM   This in't tit for tat.

HER   Feels like it.

HIM   Sorry.
I am. Sorry.
Wish I could say something
Watching your face all go like that
Honestly it's never easy for me, seeing your face go
like that.
But I just like
don't really feel like I belong here any more.

HER   Of course you do.

HIM   Well
alright.

–

HER   No wait I
We've got other things to
Let's just

Don't go just yet.
Hey. Have a look. Over here.
I'm glad you turned up with it still a bit here.
Because look there's still the ladder here from the
hayloft.
And I know we got told off for it but
You remember playing horses here?
Still smells the same here, yeah?
No wait a minute
don't
not just yet.
You want to play horses with me?
Go catching minnows in the beck?
Why did we ever stop doing that
?
We could play a game of mummies and daddies.

HIM   You know I don't like that game.

HER   What should we play then?
        Come on then I'll let you choose.

HIM   I'm going to go now.

HER   Don't go in yet.
        We've got time before we're meant to be back.
        No one's called for us.
        No one even knows we're out here.
        We could climb up in the stacks and make a nest and
        nestle down there for hours and they'd never even
        know where to find us.
        We could go out to the fields
        Or on to the foss
        We could do whatever you like.

        –

        No.
        Don't go.
        Not just yet.
        Come and sit here beside me and just
        Close your eyes.

        –

Remember that feeling like
Smell in the hay
Listen to just the blackbirds and probably a tractor
couple of fields away.
It's summer and it's still quite warm.
We got a bit wet playing by the beck
and the sun's going a bit
so there's just a slight chill now and so
You put your arm round me.
–

And I'll put my head on your shoulder.
Stay just a bit longer
with me
here.

A Nick Hern Book

Blackthorn first published in Great Britain in 2018 as a paperback original by Nick Hern Books Limited, The Glasshouse, 49a Goldhawk Road, London W12 8QP, in association with InSite Performance and Leeds Playhouse

Blackthorn copyright © 2018 Charley Miles

Cover image: © shutterstock.com/Andrija Markovic

Designed and typeset by Nick Hern Books, London
Printed in Great Britain by Mimeo Ltd, Huntingdon, Cambridgeshire PE29 6XX

A CIP catalogue record for this book is available from the British Library

ISBN 978 1 84842 779 2